I.   *For the Delicate*

You are untarnished by the world
You are placed in the center of each road
marking opposite directions;
always indecisive of which way to go.

You are standing on the corner
with your unstained white sneakers
your mom purchased for you last Christmas.

You wonder if the longer you stare
at the girl at the grocery store
if she will notice you too.

You question the smallest details -
the significant fragments of each figure
roaming through the aisles, the parks,
the restaurants and you attempt to process
if you are the only eight-year-old who
feels alone in a crowded room so you
observe every single human.

You distract yourself in the laughter,
the humor of moments that don't make
sense.

You give comfort to those who can't help
but to ask why you were so silent.

Little did they know your mind
was a restless circuit of every bottled fear
that you will never be more than
just the girl who was too quiet.

/ *I was always the listener*

"Make a wish!" my mom would inspirit
as she leaned over my shoulder.
Hesitantly, I bit my tongue and
glared at every single relative in the room.

I can't tell you how many times
I watched time stop for a moment or two.

Year after year and I captured
the expressions of every face growing
except for my will to cherish
the times when life kept moving forward.

I would wish for the world to stop
I would beg for the weather to stay warm
I would plead for a sister to hold
and maybe another barbie doll
Ask either my mother or father

Tell them I blew out every candle
with the intention of having the ability
to jump through time and space
instead of worrying about the future -

Instead of dreaming of the day
I would make it someday.

/ Tell them I just wanted to be okay.

I was exactly four years old
when you were suddenly born
into this world and I knew from the
start that I wanted nothing
more than to make certain
every significant moment
I spent boring you with my favorite
tv show you probably will roll
your eyes over once you read this poem
and smile because you know exactly which
one I'm talking about those nights we
shared pillow fights during those
countless sleepovers.

You were my once every year wish
I whispered to myself each year
I blew out the birthday candles.
I considered you my only chance
at getting a little sister -
from the days we shared those moments
playing in piggy piles,
dancing on swing sets and
the backs of grocery carts,
to the handwritten letters
and outstanding amount of
unfinished coloring books -

We got older, and it was sad to see us drift apart when I began to pivot more about my obsession with staying inside the lines of my portrait, idealizing myself as this girl who could always be better for those I loved.

I spent too much energy trying to make it perfect because I never understood what it was like to be given directions to self-love, and self-appreciation

Therefore, I tell you this in desperation to believe that from experience, before you let yourself slip and fall into the traumatic self-resentment one fails to find themselves already trapped in, the moment you start to make the same mistakes I did, conjuring up those lies you keep telling yourself that you are not good enough or you are not worth it until you are someone else's idea of perfection, I want you to know that

You are nothing but irrevocably
beauteous to me.

Please believe that you are worthy,
You are more than ordinary,
You are here, and you are free
to be just as lovely as the little sister
 I always dreamed
would live a better life than me.

/ *You are perfect to me.*

The first time I was face to face with
a professional nutritionist; I was eleven.
I sat there on that clay painted leather bed,
and she asked me why I was here.
I shrugged my shoulders,
revealing the words
I just want to be beautiful.

She guided me to the scale,
lifting both feet onto the stool,
I felt the tears form soon enough
when she retorted the concern
that I was already perfect for my age.
I convinced her to give me a sheet
of healthy meals to eat, but within the next
few weeks, I forced myself to stop eating
because nothing was rather excessively
loathsome than staring at my reflection in
the mirror.

I could make this poetic, hell,
I could create a piece of art out of this,
But as an eleven-year-old girl,
struggling to find comfort in her own cells
the next six years, I wanted to reassure
the words to any other girl going through
this -

You are not the size of your clothing,
You are not defined by the insults every fake
friend tends to propose like a fashion trend,
You are not made to listen to them.

You are not the calories consumed
in that muffin.
You are not less than any carb,
fat, or grams of sodium.
You are not made to be just a pretty face
for anyone's consult or admiration.

You are more than the scars you drew
those nights the crickets wouldn't leave you
be, you are more than worthy of every tear
you shed questioning what was ever wrong
with your body.

You are more than every unfitted bikini,
more than every self-deteriorating diary
you kept stored beneath your endless stories
of wanting to be somebody.

Sweetheart face the truth
embrace the curves and the quirks,
the shapes and milestones it took
forming every stretch mark
that you must never be ashamed of.

These bones you have are no longer weak,
the heart that beats is yours to keep
and I beg of you to keep trying to breathe
even when it feels like you're too fatigued.

You are more beautiful than any
photoshoot in a magazine,
You are more unique than any debilitating
soul who attempts to crush your self-worth
any longer -

You are lovely,
You are holy,
You are blemished with
your own particular kind of wonderful,

And I hope you know that
there is more to life than counting calories,
sore ankles and dry throats,
skin and bone -

You are constructed to be louder
than the ghosts in your head
who took over you before.

I hope you learn to love them,
because if they never were heard,
You wouldn't be capable of being
the queen of your own self-contempt
kingdom you built out of bricks and stones
from all of those who broke you prior.

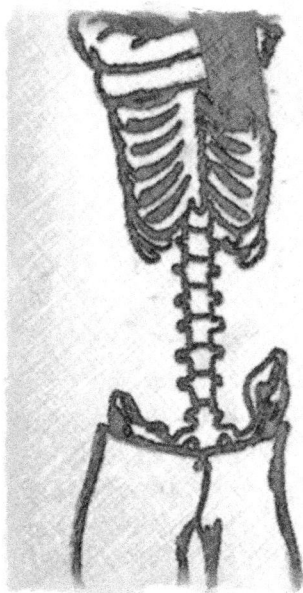

/ *You are more than your eating disorder.*

When I was a little girl,
I had this pin straight chestnut brown hair,
practically almost black and I had
this irrevocable fear of chopping it.

When I was a little girl,
I had this repugnance for cough medicine
and I guess that is why I always threw it up
because I didn't mind jacking up
my body temperatures to 102 fevers.

When I was a little girl,
Since being four feet tall,
my mom told me that I also
had this infelicitous habit of
touching an extensive amount
of hot surfaces -

Once I was told I somehow placed
the palms of my hands above the steam
exhaling from a humidifier until
I started screaming.

Once was that one specific time
my mom and I were cooking
another one of my favorite pasta dishes
and as soon as she turned around,
I dipped my fingers in the broiling water.

Not to mention the purposeful attempt
of sneaking in her bedroom
enticed by the shimmer of the metal side
of an iron, but last but not least
every single one of my family members
never fails to overlook the innumerable
amount of times I set my entire hands
on top of the wires above the oven
we had back then not once, but twice –
She made it obnoxiously clear to stay away
from the things that would hurt me.
No matter how many visits to the ER
No matter how many fits and tantrums
I cried out for her, I still never listened
anyway, did I?

/ *Maybe that's why I always
went after the bad guys.*

You were so picky about what you ate
and your mother blamed it on your
obsession with the taste of ramen and
buttered pasta -
but little was she aware that most nights
you dumped it out, if not, you left those
imprints of your fingernails
when you scratched at the rolls on your
stomach for getting too big
like the cinnamon rolls
she joyfully made after stating
how enthusiastic she was about watching
another one of your favorite horror films.

Except all you wanted to tell her was how
you could not rid the anxiety of being
confronted by the snakes that hissed at you
every single day at the lunch tables,
always prompting you to keep
that stomach of yours on empty
or else nobody would be subtle enough
to talk to you.

The best part about that whole year,
was you still convinced yourself that
these people were your friends.

/ *Friends don't make you play pretend.*

Maybe next time I cross paths
with another enchanting garden
I will make an effort to keep distance
between some of the enticing roses
that secretly have been poisoned
with that mistaken color of red
instead of green that forms on the leaves,
since I can't seem to stop catching
an unfortunate case of poison ivy
every time I come face to face
with another somebody.

In hopes this time, I won't have to
remember all the ways you hardly hesitated
to reassure me that I would never
be good enough for anybody.

/ *I am not made to be beautiful for you.*

I have come to the point in my life where
people come and people go.

Like an endless stream of ghosts
who believe they can saunter
throughout the hallways,
flickering the lights and creaking
floorboards

I have made it pretty clear that I am
tired of watching people take advantage
that this house I call my home
is not made for casual walk ins,
and unapologetic welcomes

When you were the one who found it
easy to slam the doors the times
I settled for less than a hello.

/ *I am not made to live in fear*
that you will not come back anymore.

Call me the world's biggest hypocrite.
Perhaps I shall be nominated for
the world's best award for being culpable
in letting the past characters
in the one too many disastrous love stories
make themselves at home when a year later
comes around and I cannot bring myself
to decline their phone call or voicemail
of asking me if I am doing alright after all
this time.

Sometimes, I am the character who
cannot help but be the one to initiate it first.

Because I am the world's largest failure
at holding grudges because I can't figure out
rubix cubes, or tie my shoelaces
like everyone else -

I can't react to those stupid jokes,
I can't watch a dramatic tv show
for too long, I can't drive in silence
without thinking about everything
in life that is going all wrong

I end up leaving an apologetic
message as if I was the one
projecting myself in the wrong-doing.
I end up writing myself
as the blame taker,
thinking if I just rinsed the ice
stained on my windshield that it'd
be easier to see clearer;
but you can't drive before
you let a car defrost –

You can't remove the stains
on your own just because you miss the
sound of the voice, telling you that
you are still a thought
that crosses their brain,
because no matter what the story dictates,
the story between the both of you
was already over from the beginning.

/ *Stop trying to rewrite a better ending.*

There has always been a part of me
missing, like I have been living in
the center of different segments
to the puzzle designated to create
a destination of happiness within myself.

I have been pacing back and forth
on eggshells and shreds of glass
of blown out light bulbs it seems
just to feel a sensation beneath my feet.

I have come to realization that these
damages will no longer recover if I
insist to keep picking the wrong puzzles
just because I am too fatigued to figure out
my own.

I think it's time I find solitude within
the sections of this art I call my home.
I want to question if that is even attainable,
but nothing is inevitable.

I deserve to be content, and whole
without the hands of another
soul that only provides me with
what if's and maybe's

/ *I deserve to have something*
more than temporary

You are in the passenger seat of the vehicle
you have spent these past few decades
gazing at the beautiful boy of your dreams
to enunciate the words that you are more
than just the girl who laughed at his
tedious jokes, or his abundant stories.

He would go on for hours, it seemed
to try to impress you that he was
nothing less than an intelligent soul
with the eyes of unsafe driver
since you still found yourself
reaching for his hand the nights
he wasn't there

But you were still fastened in your seat belt
making comfort with the sounds of
all the incredible ways he gave you credit
for being able to stay alive upside down.

/ *He was never worth the ride.*

If only I had known that I deserved more
than just a one-time ticket to the carnivals
of amusement rides and rollercoasters,
If only I had payed attention to the friends
disguised as the operators who check
to be sure you wear your seatbelt.
If only I was aware that all the games of
shooting darts and throwing hoops
that earned you a significant souvenir
at the end of them would determine
that this amusement park would last
more than a few hours, because that is what
I have learned to adjust to when meeting
someone.

It is all fun and games,
fireworks and photobooths
ice cream cones and fried dough,
It is all exhilarating to have
that someone appreciate you
in those first and foremost moments
until the ride is over
and you must go home to return
to whether you are worth
a second phone call,
or if you're lucky, another rollercoaster.

/ *The afterthoughts of first dates.*

You should not have to guard yourself.
You should not have to pretend that
you are just irreproachable enough to be
just a simple text message that you
wonder if you're even worth getting a
response to.

You should not have to filter what is eating
away at you when he smirks at you in that
one specific way where you can feel your
insides begin to thaw out when he only
reaches his hand over to embrace you,
but little is he aware you went home
imagining if you had just made
that one first move.

You should not have to feel stupid,
or guilt ridden to have these feelings
that you have to keep forcing to stay inside
this coffin you built the day you met him -

Because you are too consumed
in the fears that if he were to find out,
you would be nothing but a historical fact
that nobody finds the effort to keep learning,
so they close the book because they
have better things to do than
make up their mind if you
are genuinely worth pursuing.

If you have these doubts in your brain,
if you cannot distract these thoughts about
what if's and is it ever going to happen?

Newsflash, it won't be any sort of happily
ever after until you realize that
overshadowing every red flag
and every intersection
telling you to find someone better
that places you in the passenger seat
instead of the back, or the trunk -

You are more than a second choice.
You are more than just
having the power of invisibility.

/ Stop settling as a friend.

My mother and I have come down to
an understanding of the perfect metaphor
of my dating life -

You know, how every lover I seem
to get increasingly attached to
starts to fleet too soon
like the amount of time it takes before the
nail polish starts to chip off my fingernails.

The quicker I observe the paint
disintegrate from each finger
is the reason why I now decide to keep
a permanent bottle of nail polish remover.

It is intriguing, however,
the way toxic love compels us to keep
brushing over the blemishes
off the nails that were destined to diminish

Yet we keep convincing ourselves
despite the amount of coats we continue
to keep placing over it,
somehow toxicity between two people
will become normal.

/ *This is why I only allow myself clear coats.*

My creative writing teacher back in senior
year had this belief that talking about things
expressing your deepest, darkest secrets
was a way to acknowledge the grief
one has dealt with.

Although she had a point,
I was always a stubborn one
when it came to the fear of judgement
so I always kept it bottled inside until she
instructed this assignment of comparing
ourselves to a bucket or a shovel.

You see, people are often
raised to be shovels.
They are able to dig themselves out, even
when they accidentally or purposefully dug
themselves in.

Shovels are the easy way out.
They are useful for building sand castles
and paving maps to coat yourself in them -
a representation of a stable person
who can accept the bad with the good,
but then there is me -

I am the bucket that takes in all of it.
While people keep pouring every
story, every laugh, every secret, and every
heartfelt moment I keep hoarded in the
nostalgic sections of my head -
So I write them down in all the journals
I keep hidden on my third bookshelf.

However, I didn't ask for this gift
intentionally - for this bucket
may be full of treasures,
it also never gets emptied
but continues building
until I have no more to take

So I am left by the ocean
forsaken with words and flashbacks of those
who left me here when they no longer
needed me to begin with.

/ I can't tell you how many times
I have tried to be a shovel.

We were sitting approximately five feet
from each other on opposite ends of your
sofa, watching another gruesome one of
your favorite horror films –
I believe called A House of 1000 Corpses.
And as I strived to pay attention to this
graphic movie,
engaging myself to perceive one character
find amusement in slicing up the other,
I almost choked on my cup of frozen
mangos when you uttered the words
'I love you" out of nowhere.

My first instinct was to channel out
the words I almost predicted as something
I had conjured up in my own head,
so I proceeded to ignore them just before
you happened to repeat yourself, again.
"I love you."
I swallowed, gradually making eye contact
with you, and the only question
I could think to respond was,
"What do you mean?"
You said,
"I just love everything about you."

/ *Memories I Cannot Forget Pt. I*

Backyards, and stone walls
to plastic car beds and church bells -
Your first love is that reminder
of every single numbered days
it took for you to get over the fact
you knew he deserved better.

Shared milkshakes, and tickle fights
to the long walks and sleepless nights;
You spent that summer glued to his side
because you knew anywhere else
wasn't as contempt
than being able to see his smile ignite.

Laundromats, and late-night carnivals
to crystal lakes and school field trips -
You knew you were falling too fast
but part of you wanted to make it last
because the dreadful weeks it took for me to
leave my bed after I lost you
were the nights I prayed it would
make sense to me someday
why I did what I had to do.

There was no question to be asked
if I was confronted with the concern if
I had ever loved you -
because they say if you love someone,
you can love them enough to let them go.

Four years down the road,
I figured maybe it would be a different
story, except it was a little bit funny
how my best friend stumbled across
my one and only ineradicable love story.

A love story I may never forget,
but in these circumstances I will now
always be reminded of my first taste
from what love is supposed to feel like.

Even when the person
you can fall in love with
deserves to be with someone so much better.

/ I hope you fell in love with her too.

I kind of just want a person.
I want to wear someone's large sweatshirt.
soaking myself in the scent
of their laundry soap.
I want to binge-watch our favorite tv shows
I want to stroll through the towns local parks
with their arm around my shoulder
and I'll persuade them to take cute photos
with my polaroid pictures.
I want someone to exhale their warm breath
onto my fragile trembling fingers
and hold theirs against my lips when we go
for long drives with no destinations.

I want to keep them as my lucky charm
I want to store them in my bookshelves of
all my favorite stories
I want to bake pumpkin bread
and chocolate cupcakes
covering our faces in flour and lick the cake
mix off each other's fingers.

I want to know their ticklish spots.
If they keep the hallway light on or off
because they never got over their childhood
fear of sleeping in the dark.
I want to wake up to them admiring the
sound of them sleeping, their eyelids rapidly
moving as they're dreaming.
I want to be able to embrace them
and feel their heart beating.
I want to have pillow fights at midnight,
tell each other drunk stories pouring out how
irrevocably I am in love with them at 3 am.
Most importantly, I want to place my lips
upon theirs whether it's on New Year's Eve
when the clock strikes twelve,
or under the mistletoe.
I want to build snowmen on our front porch,
I want to sip hot cocoa, watch our noses run,
attempt to French kiss with crispy tongues.
I want them to know that I will forever
remain their best friend as much as their
partner who will never fail to reassure them
that I will be eternally grateful
to have fallen in love with them.

/ I hope I find you someday.

"Have you ever had your heart broken?"

Exactly three days into communicating after
we first exchanged dialed phone numbers.
Not to mention it is close to 1 am
and I can't keep my eyes open,
but you suddenly approached me with that
tenderhearted question

"I like to believe in good things,
but it's as if good things never
tend to stay with me."
I responded with the addition of stating,
"So I wouldn't say my heart is broken,
just too strung out to even play anymore."

He said, "You are very hesitant to put your heart fully into something because you already are convinced that nothing is bound to last."

I find it astonishing three days in – you haven't even met me in person, you already have me figured out more than every past lover has initiated into identifying.

/ 1 am conversations

We stayed up until the hours of dawn,
as we reluctantly lay beside one another.
Our unclothed bodies across the bed sheets
while our hearts revealed every buried
thought only due to the face that
we knew when the sun came up,
we would nowhere be found
in the same life afterward.

He would spit out of the words
as if it was something he was afraid
of bringing up,
"Are you a sad person?"
I would answer, "Why would I be sad?"
"You don't seem to like talking
about yourself; you don't like
to depend on anybody."
"I don't think there's anything
wrong with that."
"Do you ever let anyone in?
Do you ever let anyone really see you?"
"What's the point anyways?
It never lasts long enough for me to try."

That's when he pulled me close enough
to feel the heartbeat against his chest
upon my back where we embraced one
another removing any sudden thought
about how tragic it was to be stuck
in a world where we spoke
from closed out hearts
and clogged arteries
of the lovers who left
imprints previously.

I just find it funny
the first night we met,
you didn't even need a microscope
to catch every embellished mark
I present to most men.

You were probably just like me,
and that's something I will
never quite understand.

/ Memories I Cannot Forget Pt. II

So it seems the first night we crossed paths,
we shared three more adventures
with your hand in mine, strolling past
shopping malls after wrong exit turns,
guideless traffic and aesthetically pleasing
stores containing specifically detailed
scented perfumes leather carved notebooks,
and books with no covers

It seems the universe may have
intertwined us perhaps in a different time
zone because I can't help but resemble
myself when I feel your endearing gaze
when I look around at the places
we've sauntered through

I am compelled to take risks with you.
Curving our smiles into photographs
that we capture the days the world
disappears and it's only us
wandering this earth

From dusk until dawn, I remain
guarded as the only brave soul
who attracts the same as her own,
and maybe that's why I am almost terrified
of sabotaging something good for once

Because I am convinced I have met you
before in more than just that particular
bookstore, the place we dipped
our spoons in frozen yogurt,
in more than those countless coffee shops,
cemented sidewalks and our favorite films,
in more than just first tastes of cheesecake,
tai ice cream and
chocolate covered strawberries

You are the bittersweet memory
I want to keep remembering.
You are the soul I want to keep admiring
for choosing to fall for a girl like me.

/ *But I wasn't the right one*

"Why are you upset?" He asked.
"I just don't want to lose you."
"I told you, I'm not going anywhere."
She wept, "I never thought I was worth
finding someone like you."
He whispered, "I don't understand why you
wouldn't think you never were.
Because you deserve nothing but the world,
and I'm going to do everything
in my power to give that to you.
I promise no matter what happens, I will
always find my way back to you."
"Are you going to stop me
if I wait for you?"
"No."
"Good, because you're worth the wait."
"Am I now?"
"Definitely."
She leaned forward to kiss him,
in the matter of a few seconds
it began to feel like forever.
He kissed her forehead, and wrapped his
arms, embracing her closer.

/ *Memories I Cannot Forget Pt. III*

You always did that;
You always found your way into making
things romantic
from the hand-written letters
to the vanilla scented candles
to the candy bars and glass roses
you left in my mailbox that time
I caught my eye on the words taped back
to it that represented forever in the matter of
a few seconds -
like that time you wrapped me in your
blanket or when we made hot cocoa in your
mother's kitchen.
We attempted to watch the grinch stole
Christmas right around the then and I
remember how we sat by your fireplace,
throwing our deepest buried secrets traced in
pencil inside random sticky notes into the
flames of every bad thought and decisions
we ever made.

*Like we hadn't expected the rest of
what we had to do the same.*

It has been approximately 365 days and let
me just state that no matter how tragically
we fell into our separate ways,
I hope you found a better way to sleep with
the memories of us somehow being destined
to find our way back together

I can't tell you how many times I have
wished on shooting stars that I wanted to
believe I deserved someone
as generously compassionate as you.

I find myself strolling through train stations
and bicycle paths even boardwalks to
hopefully stumble across somebody
who not just sees me, but looks at me in a
way where I am not just someone you can
undress but willing to reveal the curtains
placed in front of my eyes
from being too damn stubborn to realize
that I deserve to be loved just as much as
every other human being on this earth.

I didn't used to know that before
when you stayed up listening to every
thought I let creep between my bones
every night I allowed myself start to
crumble when I was too selfish
to understand that you needed me
more than I needed you.

We were practically a lesson learned
while in the process of rebuilding what
could've been instead of
what it actually was and maybe
that's why I haven't heard from you
in months because I am still
too god damn selfish to come to terms
that losing you wasn't my fault.

Because it was.
Whatever that reason was,
or whatever that reason may be

I hope you learn to be happier
without me.

/ *Dear Forbidden Lover Pt. 1*

I took a risk of joining one of my closest
friends by hopping on the bus with the rest
of the crowd that week we spent our summer
in church camp.

We were surrounded by an elegant view of
the lake, amongst the trees in the woods we
hiked every morning after lunch, and I
remember at points feeling out of place.

Everyone around me had this idea that God
was the love of their life, their heart, and
savior, and then there was me who was
stranded in the forest pretending that I
wasn't stranded.
Of course, there was my best friend,
the ear I turned to, the shoulder to lean on,
vice versa, but she at least had this theory
that there was a god up above looking down
on her the nights she felt hopeless as a child,
but you see -
I was raised with a religious father and
my mother who grew wrathful at the idea of
God, and going to church,
so we never went.

For a second, however, I liked to believe
maybe there was something out there
higher than any human soul on this earth
that had placed us on this journey of finding
ourselves in desperate hopes that he knows
what we are capable of.

Except I have learned that
I don't need to go to church.
I don't have to pray.
But I acknowledge in my heart,
that there is a possibility that
there is a such thing as
life and death, love and hate,
fate and coincidence.
But I do not trust in
any good, or bad thing.

No demons, or angels.
No heaven, no hell.

I strongly believe in something out there
perhaps observing us as fragile creatures
as we are, to see the strength
we don't see in ourselves sometimes.

/ *I am agnostic.*

Last night we studied the curves of our
smiles beneath the covers, exchanging
bashful grins with the flickering light of
your television and for once in my life, all
we did was crave the intimidation of ruining
the moment with the effort of making a
move too sudden was
almost scarcely excruciating.

You told me about your one and only first
love, how she betrayed your trust in an act
of lust and I pondered if she was the reason
you kept yourself at edge the days
we shared the same shifts

Some days you would even
stop and smell the trees.
Other days you wouldn't even
dare to notice me.

Somehow, I still detect that small ounce of
anticipation to keep rewriting all the ways
we could have met instead.

Call the shots of our predestined history
as the case of two personal interests
stuck in purgatory.

I was always waiting for you to make the
first move that night we laid beside each
other, the nights I cuddled against your
shoulder the first night we met where we
talked until 4 am, sharing our interests
about poetry
and our favorite CD's
first loves and
childhood stories

But it's been over a year now since we
shared what was fate resigning our histories
of misdrawn sparks to the fires that kept us
coming back to trying again, as if each time
we kept starting off fresh would result in a
better ending of being more
than just someone you felt
compelled to talk to every now and again

/ *I wish I knew what it meant to you.*

It is an understatement of all the ways
I have been refilling slept in eyeliner
from the night before I happened
to face my reflection
and question what I am doing
with myself

It is an understatement for all the ways I
must keep taking that same road we drive
down where I subconsciously
find myself looking for your car, even when
you've been gone for over three months
now, but I still ponder if you think
about me and all the ways I must be doing
better off.

It is an understatement that when I stroll
through grocery aisles that I don't check
each one of them thinking maybe we could
so happen bump into each other

It is an understatement that every single
morning I have to retell myself that it is
never going to happen despite to objectified
flashbacks every time I envision
us crossing intersections
every now and again

As winter comes crawling
around its corners, I admit that
not only has love been the frostbites
that sink themselves in my skin,
But it is also the everlasting practicality
that I may for once feel something different.

/ But I never do.

I have been flourishing the way each petal
of every one of my favorite roses has been
stretching out through my bloodstream each
time another lover has the right to
give me that single high when they first
come by. Exchanging flirtatious smirks
and humorous quirks as we glide
through the honeymoon stage.
I have been establishing to the routine of
how every time they tend to leave
when the show is over - that I am no longer
that piece of outlined cardboard that you
used to replace your last lover, or perhaps
that empty hole you've been dreading to
blemish over.

I was never one to get consumed in drugs,
but the high I would receive at first when
you first meet the way someone can bind
their soul with yours through late night car
rides, two am phone calls, the sound of their
laughter, the bickering over places to have
dinner at - I feel every ounce of the blizzard
that makes it way tornadoing around the
doorframes of my brain, circling around all
the disappointments of what to expect in
preparation that when you make your
attempt to tell me the same words
of *"It's not the right timing,"*

Those words seep into each part of my body
formulating blood clots until my fingers
no longer feel the warmth of when the lovers
I had hoped to prove me wrong turn out
the way I had expected all along

Therefore, I have adjusted to that part time
role of being just a pretty face with the let
down of never being enough to keep myself
from going numb

Instead I am the front porch you find
yourself strolling out the mornings
you keep wondering
if I was ever worth more than
a few months with the unrighteous
determination to ask me
when you have exited every back door -
how I have been since you left
six months ago

After addressing all the ways I have
consoled with my isolation -
I only hope you never fail to keep inspiring
me in hopes you will stay when you keep
figuring out all the ways that shaped me,
you will understand that giving my all to
you is challenging for me.
I will take you on breathtaking adventures.
I will wrap gifts I found
in those random department stores.
I will create you personalized mixtapes,
and take pictures of you without looking
just to keep me smiling when I cannot find
slumber but wonder how I got so incredibly
lucky to have someone to call my partner.
I genuinely hope we are still going on
spontaneous trips, holding your hand while
you drive, singing to music, going for walks,
embracing you when necessary,
but most importantly, I hope I make you
happy and not in a forceful kind of way.

If I am reading this to you, I hope you are
aware of that you are every shooting star,
every garden, every love letter I ever knelt
and prayed to have ever wanted.

/ Dear Future Lover
Please don't be like the rest of them.

II.

For the Lonely

What pains me most to say is ultimately
coming to terms that these things occur.
You cannot stop it,
You cannot run from it,
Nor can you change it.
You can just experience it.

Let yourself endure the grief,
the endless stream of tears rolling down
your cheeks. Let it out how the world seems
to be falling at your feet, and you cannot
even find a single ounce of air to breathe.
I am telling you, that even in these moments
of when your world is starting to crumble
and you have no
single soul to confide to -
you are still breathing
with a pulse and a heartbeat,
and I can guarantee that this is temporary.

So please, keep moving forward
even when it gets this unbearable.

/ *When it gets bad.*

I have raced through deserts with coarse
skin. I have sprinted through marathons of
being chased after the ghosts of those I
intended to forget, but still catch up to me
when I am finally able to embrace that small
ounce of being happy.
I have gotten one too many blisters,
suffered too many cases of sunburn
for sometimes it seems that the sun
is too scintillating that I am desperate for the
shade that coats me with a sense of safety.

I am most comfortable up in the trees
and I am most content watching how the
moon glistens behind the stars, attentive to
the howls of the wolves and the sirens of
ambulances, sounds of airplanes and tow
trucks on the highway.
Everything is silent but awakened at night
and maybe that is why my mom tells me that
I am so quiet at times that she swears
the crickets are audible, but little is she
aware that I am the owl that hovers outside
your bedroom windows always keeping to
myself in the shadows.

/ *I have always been a night person.*

I know there are days you cannot sleep
during thunderstorms since you are
so discomforted by your own resistance
to overthinking your own thoughts.
I know there are days you want to secrete
yourself underneath the covers and when
your own mother that you love with your
heart and soul cannot see that you wish to
not be bothered by the emptiness in your
eyes, the constant fixation to project a smile.
I know there are times you are so
unbalanced with the way the world you live
in is supposed to function, but you cannot
stop yourself from glaring at your bedroom
ceiling, letting time take a few moments
before picking back up, because it is in those
short amount of seconds
that not everything is not falling apart.

It is just until your body starts to tremble at
the activity of getting up, because this home
you get to live through most mornings is the
reasons why you wish it all would just stop
when the earthquake of over dwelling
thoughts starts to come back again.

/ *I was never a morning person.*

Winter has hardly come close
to the way I sympathize better
with the four different seasons.

I have always remained pale,
soft skinned - the girl with a tint of gold
that coats the iris in her eyes.

You will never find a body like mine with
temperature of lukewarm for too long
because I sense being cold blooded
prolongedly that I have gotten used to ways
the cold is the blanket I use to
make comfort with
during hibernation -

I hardly twist and turn in my sleep
I am almost like a statue it seems
drifting off into my own daydreams.

I was driving through deserted streets
passing signs and flickering stop lights
around 11pm, observing the first day
it had snowed this season.

I am not one to fantasize over the winter
but somehow, I think I have a theory
that maybe the snow is an accurate
representation of how I see at myself,
but for once
I want to feel different.

Winter has always been the
season I put up with
but never once fell in love
with the beauty of it.

/ *I wonder what that says about me.*

There are days
where being on my own seems like
my strength is just as fragile as a
glass vase containing each bouquet
of my favorite red roses.

Somedays
I am endlessly watering them.
Somedays
I am pouring too much out to refresh

Most days
I am holding each petal I spent
trimming off each of their stems,
analyzing for one too many hours
the shape of them delicately placed
in both palms of my hands.

Somedays I am not strong.
Somedays I am just barely carrying
the weight of my own strength,
this glass case when each
petal begins to look worn out

This is when I start to drown
when the world I make myself at home
is too fatigued to carry its own.

/ *The strong carry the most.*

I have always been that girl
on the back burner
I have always been the "could've been"
contemplated about the "should've been"
but was never meant to happen.

Every partner I found myself
writing about their deepest desires,
like the scent of their favorite candle
or the best tasteful chocolate bar,
their top choice of coffee,
whether they preferred cream or sugar
or maybe just all black and raw.

All I yearned was for someone
to consider that I was made more
than the girl who kept notes like
a typewriter that recorded every detailed
story you spoke to me the nights
we laughed up until 3 in the morning

It seemed after a while, despite how often
I kept track of every exquisite characteristic
about them like if winter was their favorite
season or they would rather go bowling than
ice skating

It seemed when the spring came,
It would begin to down pour progressively
until I subconsciously made it a priority to
keep watering their gardens without making
a mental note to keep mine from
saturating in their disfigured outlines
where I came to realize that love has done
nothing but abandon me with sleepless
nights because I kept assuming they would
come back if they noticed I was doing
everything in my power
to just keep the history we spent making
from flooding into the rest of the puddles
I found myself stumbling over again

/ All I wanted was to keep growing.

I counted the dimples on his face
awaiting the amount of times
we would meet again before I'd get to
watch them fade the days he neglected
to state he never planned to stay

So the moments I held him against me,
the minutes I got him to smile
that I kept treasured in my memory

These moments I keep stored
in every book case of every chapter
I spend waiting for me to run out of ink
waiting for someone to jinx
that I don't have to feel guilty for
feeling gratified after we part to reality

I told him I am not a shadow
You cannot erase my echo when I demand
of you to hold me steady instead of
closing any possibilities of better chapters -

He found it more useful to wrap me
in tissue paper, store me on the top shelf
where he warned me if I spoke more
about love and letting it take its course

I would have to find somebody else

The problem with today's century
is the second you spill too much
is the risk you make of them giving up
the times you spent exchanging gifts,
long walks and in-depth conversations

All of it is taken back
once you get too attached.

/ Filtered

And I stare at the moon
the nights I cannot sleep
the breaths I waste
and I cringe at the taste
of this whiskey

I talk to the stars
and I point to the leaves
whistling to me

I ask if there is any God listening
the only question I can manage
to speak before collapsing

When will it ever stop?

When will someone just stay?

/ Don't leave

He told me that I was just as
unique as the stars
in the galaxies he prayed seeking
the day he would end up encountering
a girl like me.

He told me that fate has its ways by
connecting the stars in the sky,
representing a sign of the right timing
as if we had our own constellations.

He told me the stories of every time
another ex-lover had showed up
in his backyard,
claiming their infatuation for him
after only a few weeks
of blatant mistrust and lack of
communication.

He told me that I was different -

So when the universe allowed our stars
to realign again, I figured what more reasons
was there to show in the world we spent
months strolling hand in hand
in grocery stores,
late night phone calls,
or watching those atrocious films
he claimed were his favorite ones -
I told him what other way does this universe
have to show him that the answers
to the question he had kept conjuring up
in his own head was
actually right in front of him?

He tells me now,
he never felt it.

/ *I like to call bull-shit.*

I'm one of those girls who
saves your text messages
when you decide to tell me something sweet.
I'm one of those girls who recollects each
time you smiled in your sleep
And I will quote each line of
which you spoke to me
just because I like the way you speak.
I'm one of those girls who will
deny that wishes on shooting stars
ever come true
but I might leave thanking you
to what love must taste like.
I'm one of those girls who is running low
on Chapstick from locking lips with too
many frogs that failed to turn into prince
charming's but I'm also one of those girls
who finds the most amusement in those
cliché movies

You know, the way how every love story
has to have a happy ending?
I'm also one of those girls who grows
extremely angry with the way a love story
can predictably end with a tragedy.

But it's just funny,
The way books and literature have a way
in general of making every one of us
come to terms of how unpredictable
romance is in this replacement of reality.

Everyone wants to find that person
to be that cleanse of coffee in the morning,
or that scent of fresh air when you step
outside but love, it seems in this generation
is something we have learned to be cautious
about. In other words, love is another game
of cops and robbers -

I remember this visual I once came across
on Tumblr portraying this girl caressing the
tip of a gun as this boy aimed it into her
mouth and in some shape way, or form
it represented how someone you can trust
can end up just dilapidating you and that's
what I am trying to make a point at -

Love is not about saving something
nor is it about giving the right to place a gun
on the tip of your tongue
But I can't deny that sometimes,
that's what it feels like.

I'm one of those girls who used to be afraid
to fall in love.

But let me tell you something,
Love is not a game of cops and robbers
it's about stepping in front of the person
worth taking a bullet from,
not when you have them wrapped around
your finger,
contemplating when it the right them to start
another game of who is better at
manipulation
because we always have that question in the
back of our heads
if love is worth fighting for so when we dare
to meet someone,
we have this endless deliberation with
ourselves if this girl or this guy
is the worth the chance of not being so
goddamn fearful
of coming face to face with another person
behind the trigger

I'm one of those girls who may still be
afraid to admit that this body of mine has
anxiety of pouring this part of earth's
creation into another awful atmosphere
because I may be strong,
but I am still vulnerable.

That does not mean I am willing to find
myself slipping into the wrong footsteps of
another one of god's creatures who
tend to look at me like I could be the smoke
that they inhale from their cigarettes because
I am not someone you can just
take back into your hollow chest when you
are too stressed out to believe that I can be
more than just secondhand smoke.

I can be one of those girls
who wraps you up in blankets
I can be one of those girls who
helps you quit your addictions
I can rid you of those bad thoughts over
again, but love, my friend is not a temporary
solution for someone's mental health
problems and I've had to learn that
the hard way.

Because at the end of the day,
you're just another creature
they make comfort with during hibernation
until next season, well excuse me for maybe
thinking once, or twice
or maybe a couple hundred times that maybe
love isn't something worth fighting for if
nobody is willing to fight for me.

I'm one of those girls who used to
beat herself down
I would build stone walls out of bricks
inside my bedroom and refuse to let another
soul make themselves at home
because sooner or later, they would find
their desires into other girls' mattresses and
I refuse to be left again to wonder
if this never-ending feeling of loneliness
would ever stop but the thoughts of them
coming back would haunt me
like the sound of a twig breaking,
and I would hear them call out for me
But I am undeniably sorry my love,
I am not the one who needed saving
in the first place.

I can't deny that some nights I had to endure
the sensation of fracturing my every bone to
sustain the hurt in their voice
that made me want to help them,
 but oh my god -
If there is one out there,
I would like to take the time
to appreciate the helping hand
throughout the dreadful piles
of chaos those boys would attempt
to leave me with inside of their heads
because I was too sympathetic
so I would listen to every
single one of them.

I used to be one of those girls
who let herself drown
in those who got to decide
when it was safe to start
taking advantage of the fact that
I was still there,
and I was still listening.
But within those dark periods of loneliness
I am proud to say that I grew into one of
those girls who learned to depend on herself;

My echo that spreads
across the country
I listen for those who
pour their heart
out to me
We are the wolves
that have been wounded to our souls
but we are the ones who will give you
everything we got until it is time for us to
leave in certain that in unfortunate
circumstances that it is a precaution
we let anyone get too close until it is their
call to confirm just how beautiful we all are

-

To the journeys we've been put through
just to make it out alive,
with our rough skin and silk fur -
We are better than those
who left us in the cold
We are those who survived
the unrealistic fairytales
and ended up risking our lives through
hurricanes of heartbreaks
We are the lovers who know
what is worth fighting for
and at the end of it all,

We have to learn to love ourselves first.
You are nobody else's but your own.

Never forget to remind yourself
that you are not alone,
even when you find yourself sleeping
on soaked pillows,
You are one and you are here
and your tears are a means
to know that you are strong and
you are worthy
of every ounce of every love letter
in the world

Listen to the wolves outside
your windows at night

We all know what it's like
to be you too.

/ *Forget The Ones That Forgot You*

Your name is like a faded echo
when I look up at the stars
and I watch each one of them glisten
as if I haven't been here before.

Your touch is just as brisk as the breeze
embracing every window while the wind
allows itself to acknowledge
my isolation the days I long for
the trees to talk back to me.

You see,
I must have been dreaming when
I carved your name in the bark,
scraping my nails across
until I no longer felt the grief of you
being gone for weeks
that led to months of me letting you be
better off as just the thoughts of you
lingering throughout my bloodstream

I had to keep reminding myself those
nights I would stay up too late
watching you choose her over me
"this was the way it was supposed to be,"
were the last words I heard you speak

But the problem is that your essence fixates
itself consuming each soul I reach;
You are the light bulb that
keeps itself flickering
until I cannot erase her from my dreams

So I attempt to carve her name beside yours
in the bark where I sit in silence
staring at the ceiling to justify why
my fingers are still bleeding

/ *Don't let me fall back in asleep*

They say if you love something,

let it go.

If it comes back, it is yours for certain -

But he was never mine,
nor was he ever good for me to begin with.

/ This is why it hurts to let go.

III.

For the Deceiving

To the boy who presented himself as an
immature 20-year-old who already forgot
his notebook, pen, and paper on the exact
first day of school, I knew the minute
I saw you that it was going to be an
interesting year.
As the weeks went on, it did not take long
before you stroked your beard the times you
could not take your eyes off me, so instead
you moved close enough to
act nicely in hopes you would
ask me out politely.
When I courteously said no, you proceeded
to follow me to the coffee shop I worked at,
with the idea that maybe I would reconsider
my options but all that led to be your
evacuation from security.

To the men who have gray hair, or perhaps
stand tall and bald,
perhaps you're almost hitting the
magnificent age of 44 -

I do not find it attractive,
much less clever to ask me out
when I was only an eighteen-year-old girl.
Do not get me started on the man who
would repetitively call my store just to talk
to me about how my day was
Or the guy who flew down from his trip in
Canada to buy me chocolate for only
recommending him a pair of black overalls

And I must not even mention the worst of
all, the guy who mistook my kindness for a
hint to persuade me into the fitting room to
make his delirious delusions come true.
To my surprise, he came back with the
intentions of asking me out on a real date
when I did not give him the satisfaction to
be alone with him, and I almost spit out
the gulp of water when he blamed it on
being "bold."

In hopes if any of you read this, you
probably don't even remember my name
but you'd probably recognize my face
because you were too busy consuming
yourself in all the dirty tricks you wish you
could do to my body. But you forgot to
register that I am still a woman who is
a human being that is not made to live up to
your misconceptions of being too friendly,
so I suggest you walk away before
you start to discomfort me with your eyes
that will start to undress me
the longer you keep staring.
So before that happens,
I will make it known that you are just as
childish than a 3-year-old
and a real woman should never settle less to
those standards.

/ *Appealing Tragedies*

93 | For Every Rose

When I think about you,
I think about that necklace in the shape
of a bird's wing that I gave to you
that Christmas eve of 2014.

I was the girl who would've crossed
the seven seas just to meet you
except you made it clear the hours I spent
after school that it was all just a game,
until you began to sing that awful song
to the siren that kept me coming back into
playing for the spot to be more than just the
girl who spent that entire year yearning for
your attention

To be more than just than girl who
suffered with her own battling
thoughts of depression,
the nights you actually answered your phone
and listened to them, holding me hostage

It was snowing that night,
almost around 4 pm.
My dad had been waiting for me to come
back while you chased me behind that
building where we stood with apprehension
in our eyes on those concrete steps –
I wonder if you remember.

Fast forward to a year later
first day back in those nostalgic halls,
We hadn't spoken all summer.
I saw you walking toward me
for the first time in awhile
and you came to tell me
the necklace had broken.

4 years down the road,
You had the audacity to approach
the girl who dreamt of the day
you noticed how beautiful I was.

/ When you stop chasing them

Forgive me, or forgive me not,
but I will not waste my tears
to form the river any longer
where I was the one left to drown
after building you a river to swim
into your happily ever after's.

These losses I have endured
have built themselves dams and sinking
ships that often eventually timber over
and I am so tremendously depleted from
attempting to rebuild what was faltered from
the start.

It is not my doing of why each time
I pass that one distinctive grocery store,
or that exact scent of your cologne
caught from a passing stranger,
or that one individual song that played
in the environment I was sauntering through.

It is not my fault for all the ways
I have to live with all the tormented
hallucinations of being with you
even after you have proven that
I am nothing but a distant outline
in your backyard of the lovers
you so easily got up and left behind.

However, I am not one anymore
to revive the skeletons in my closet
because I am now the ghost that knocks
on your window panes every night you
find yourself falling into deep slumber.
You will perhaps tremble at the thought
that the sound of that branch hitting
your bedroom window is the reminder
you should be sorry for thinking
it was nothing the night you told me
it was all a lovely misinterpretation.

*/ Maybe then you will see
what you did to me.*

Seeing me enwrapped in another boy's arms
apart from yours was the bullet to your
brain, which was ironic because you were
always the one who held the gun while
spiraling yourself in this boundless game of
pursuing the ones you couldn't have a
chance with anymore.

Chasing after you was like
purposely imprisoning myself into
a chain of spiderwebs
except it was too late the day
you somehow decided you were
too exhausted to play anymore games.

As if I asked to be a part of them,
you kept stumbling over your mistakes
when you couldn't decide which
lane to take as you swerved
back and forth until catching
around the corner the one and only girl
who stole your heart and to this day,
she remains in the driver's seat
with the permission to call you hers.

I'm not blaming either one of us anymore.
Because sometimes, no matter how badly
you want something to work out,

Fate has a funny way of displaying
that it was not destined to go anywhere.

/ *The Chase*

I want you to know that it is unbelievably
senseless how far we have come since we
made it out of those black fitted skinny jeans
laced with the silver chain in your pocket,
and my black band shirts and rubber
bracelets

I was once told opposites can attract
but they make the world's abominable
couples.

The amount of times I had to re-word
that shredded piece of advice
the countless nights I spent tracing
you out of me as if I just wanted to keep
replenishing the possibilities we were meant
for more than just late-night conversations
and midnight strolls at three am.

I wanted to believe it
didn't mean anything then
when you happened to meet her,
so I told myself I would keep holding on
with severed arms and burnt marks -
fantasizing the act of you ever coming back

But instead, you were the reason
I kept drawing one too many flashbacks
of the false scripts in result of me hating
myself for the next two years.

/ *They always get the happy endings.*

I remember the boy with blue eyes
and the distasteful mouth of cigarettes
told me that I shouldn't shove all the
bad parts in the back of my head as if
it were encased within the cabinets taped
with the words written in bold black ink
DO NOT OPEN.

We had spent the past few weeks
driving behind plazas, and working
together at the same job, sneaking out
behind the shed to share the drugs
that we both used to sustain our distractions
the nights we explored our sexual intentions.

And he had the audacity,
after the few hours I spent admiring
his priceless harmonies to his favorite song
that played on 93.7

He had the presumption to believe
that just because we were car buddies,
or the few slight smirks across
the kitchen we were forced to cook in,
or the late-night strolls
through department stores
that I would be more than willing
to open them up for him
when he didn't hesitate to state that
we were still "best friends."

/ *You don't get to expose me like that.*

You have this carelessness to you
that you project as if the drugs you take
make you seem incautious of the ability to
feel anything more than happiness.
But the thing is whenever I mentioned the
word depression, you passed it off like it is
something you have to run from.
I get it with the way you were raised
during your childhood.
I would do what I could to suppress any
kind of emotion except I used to feel that
way, and it was an unfortunate set back to
hear you say that just because I come here
for one thing determines that I am a woman
with no self-respect.

There was a time when I was younger,
and I found myself falling asleep in other
boys' beds as if the hours we spent
cocooned in each other's arms meant more
than just friends with benefits.

For years it seemed, I would anathematize at
the sky for me being the only one growing
vines out of my upper things when they
could never recognize the mask I placed
in desperation as a helpful cry.

Of course they never did
because it's like that phrase -
Boys will be boys.
But they forgot to mention that
girls can be girls when it comes to
a supposed over dramatic presentation
of our emotions because that's what
society expects from us.
Except the thing is now
I am built out of stone walls and cold bricks
that I formed so I don't allow myself to be
touched anymore in ways that are
no longer emotional.

So when your body is too stressed out
to keep composure - when the drugs tend to
make their adrenaline rush throughout your
blood and the thoughts start to become a
series of lovely endorphins when I make my
way into tracing my fingertips along your
sides of your hips that keep you from falling
off the railings - I ask of you not to question
the marks I left on my skin because I am my
own kingdom of catastrophe that
I made comfort with.

/ *Damaged goods.*

Fogged windows traced with our
fingerprints clouding the outlines that
allowed us to intertwine the first night I
crossed your mind

We made it far enough to park behind the
lake glistening beneath the stars,
the crickets and comforting silence
that echoed around your car

Inside we found ourselves embracing
the delicate sound of Ed Sheeran's album.
Staying up until 4 in the morning,
cracking jokes and building chemistry,
gentle embraces and innocent gazing
I felt each goose bump form on your skin
along with the curve of your smile
that I no longer seem to forget
the nights I glance at my own reflection.

The words you spoke were like
treacherous rain drops that trickled down
your windshield the nights we spent more
than tasting each other breath,
reciting every word from the script
it seemed every time we held each other for
more than ten minutes, that
We could never be more than this.

I wish I knew what you meant
I wish I could comprehend this entire
foreign language every guy I happen to meet
speaks as if it is supposed to make sense
when they find someone appealing -

As if it were to be any different
despite the same beginning
to every undeniable love story
I keep stumbling into -

Funny thing is I never asked to play the part
I never gave you permission to call me *yours*
the nights we spent too long beneath
silk sheets in hotel rooms,
late night phone calls
every once in a blue moon

I can honestly state that for once
I never questioned what I was doing
the mornings I would wake up beside you

Most times it felt like I was just
waiting for the paint to start to drip
from the decorative ceilings

From my ignorance once remembering
I was forbidden to feel a thing for you

For all I knew,
I noticed how you hid from the truth
about being cold when it came to love,
showing me wedding videos
and revealing parts of you
that no one else cared to figure out.

As if it wouldn't have hurt
to have left you behind
after finding happiness with
another who never made me
walk between the lines
of any chapter I wasn't able to write -

I beg of you to leave my mind
I sometimes talk to the walls at night
since you won't dare to reply -

Tell me now,
Why are you still haunting me
through the songs you described
on every late-night drive?

Tell me why
I still dream of your body
consuming mine with every
integrity that we were meant
for more than apologies

Tell me do you miss the taste
of my lips, the tenderness of my skin?

Maybe if you spoke clearer,
Maybe if you had better intentions,
I wouldn't have second guessed
a word you mentioned the last conversation
we bickered about our true colors
that leaked too many stains around
for us to do nothing but soak in them.

/ *Hypocrites*

You have knocked over cups of water
that have spoiled over the floorboards,
You have timbered buildings of bricks
that have come tumbling down before,
You have shattered every single back door
searching the desire to keep yourself
strolling back repeatedly as if this time
it would mean something.

The walls inside this home I made,
I have freshly painted colors
I am not used to.
I am the designer of my own catastrophe
that I spent months making excuses that
there were such things as second chances

Except I made certain to keep the walls
soundproof when you kept pleading
me to come back for you,
the glass windows indestructible when
I turned away while endeavoring
to shove your hand through.

I have polished the floors and I have taped
the words into every section of my brain
that I do not mind if you keep trying
to stamp your contaminated footprints
onto the doormat because I have taught
myself that I deserve healthier hearts
that no longer fool me with
treacherous smiles and
unfaithful words.

/ *You never deserved me,*
and you never will.

"You know that seems to be
your favorite word, **jinx**."
"I'm just saying things may be good now,
But you never know what would happen."
"You're not jinxing anything."
You assured me.
"You say that now,"
I teased before you responded with,
"And I'll say it every two weeks."

I wanted to tell you that I told you so
even before you wrapped me in your arms,
twirling me around as you danced to Frank
Sinatra outside in the parking lot where we
collided in the dark, beneath the stars that
stood beyond the moon and we confessed
that yours was the full, but mine was the
crescent because I always
had a part of me that I kept guarded.
So even when I wanted to believe
that you were different,
I had almost planned on that night being
the last time I would spot your face
a month after you ridiculed me for
my apprehension of jinxing things.

/ Now you know why.

"Was it all bullshit?"
"What do you mean?"
"I was there with you through everything,
How could you not see how long
I had waited only for you to do nothing?"
"Is that what you think? That I did nothing?"
"She didn't do anything to fight for you.
That's bullshit."
"It's not bullshit, Belle. It's just how it
worked out."

You told me that one time in that bookstore,
this time we would make it right.
To my concern, the last time I got to see
you, you were embracing that new pup of
yours wandering through that store we met.
I could feel my heart practically erupting
through my chest, and my face burning to
red contemplating how you even managed
the risk of facing me after we had just
previously argued about your encounter with
someone else –

I remember the night I stayed over your
house and we stood outside in the freezing
cold, face to face on your front porch,
talking about how the stars must make sense
for the way the world connects us
to become who we are

I couldn't help but fall for the integrity
you spoke with behind that smirk that
ignited in between the darkness of your eyes

Through the long drives,
Late night diner runs, the tickle fights,
the strolls through department stores,
It began to settle into the deepest pits
of my stomach that maybe it was
all worthless the days you would go on
for weeks without contacting me
that I meant nothing
but an inconvenience because
I begged you for consistent reassurance.

There is so much that I wish
I could say to you.
Somehow I know that if I ever
got the chance to
I would present a facade like I always do
pretending that I am so happy for you.

Maybe I'm wrong about her,
But aren't I always right when it comes to
every lover I start to fall for that leaves me
abandoned in the rivers and gardens I dug
through just to figure out that love is just
another cold sore?

I've widened my eyes to see the bigger
picture and it's not all about fairytales
and wedding rings and rose petals,
my friend,
even if you are getting married now.

I don't believe love is existent
for me anytime soon.
In the meantime, I am the observer.
I give, I take, I listen, I play.

I won't apologize for remaining as confident
as the lonely soul you could never
locate lost in her own world designed with
the most tragic pieces of art and song lyrics.
I don't mean to feel this empty sometimes,
my love, it's just something
I've grown fond of.

After everything has been set in stone -
wishing the best for you would
in this case, be my form of bullshit
no matter if we were meant to make it or
not, you were never mine to begin with.
I have no say in regards in how I felt
when in reality I was nowhere near first
place, and always settled to be a second
choice.

Your whole infatuation with fate laying out
the chapters of your life are a twisted kind of
debate because pardon me, I am convinced
fate is just an excuse
to escape the endless fight it took for me
to eventually figure out that it was all me
just fixating the wrong pieces of a puzzle to
fit right.

/ *Please don't come back again.*

It wasn't like me to have so easily let you in.

For I beg your pardon,
I swore to myself that I would no longer
want to be that girl fearful of taking risks
of falling apart if things ended,
except it was that one night we spoke over
the phone, the night that flipped how I felt
upside down as I began to pace repetitively
across my bedroom floor until 4am.

After weeks of strolls through the parks,
lunch dates and disposable films,
facetime sleepovers and meaningful looks
the days I would find my soul falling deep
for yours, I couldn't help but overlook the
mud puddles I struggled to step out of when
she placed her lips onto yours that night you
played truth or dare leading up to your
excuse of "I don't feel anything for you
anymore," as you cracked on your words,
struggling through tears.

Pardon me for misunderstanding,
Pardon me for never seeing it coming
the weeks after it all boiled over,
and the truth came out like black paint
you poured all over my window sills.

Pardon me,
maybe you were not ready
to fall for a girl like me.

I know I'm not one capable of easily
finding a person worth calling my own
definition of home. But pardon me,
I was fooled the days I decided to let you
inside without being warned if you would
ever question if you should go

If you had no intention on staying
the first night we met, then maybe you
should've thought twice the moment you
asked me to promise you to stay safe the
night you buried me in your coffin.

/ (*Pardon Me*) *for letting you in.*

To the girls who told me that I
was too repulsive to be glanced at,
that day we took a field trip
and you dared me to expose myself
in front of all of our classmates.

To the girls who insinuated that due to my
lack of ability to brush my hair,
or wear leggings instead of short shorts,
I hope you know it is not me
risking the possibility of being
pregnant at 15.

To the boy who dared to ask me,
my first crush in the fourth grade,
getting up and exiting the doorway
the minute I retrieved the note
of how I wasn't worth a second look
that afternoon in Ms. Weiner's classroom;

I'm sorry a girl like me wanted to be noticed
by a guy like you because I couldn't adjust
to the realization that I wasn't good enough
for the next three years, but made the perfect
spot to be humiliated the days I spent talking
to the swing sets if I could be prettier

To the girls who told me
that maybe if I cut my hair,
Maybe if I dressed better,
Maybe if I spoke more,
Maybe if I ate less,
Maybe if I tried less
to be so desperate for attention
instead of fixing my appearance,
that maybe I would be just as
popular as the girls who played sports,
with their bouncing pony tails,
and their attractive curves,
and their effortless talent
to get cute boys
to like them -

I hope you know
that it is not me anymore
who is still hating herself
for who she has become.

/ 10 years later.

I have been picked,
I have been used,
I have taken,
And I have been bruised
From the spots colored
From violet to blue,
I am covered in pieces
of all the hints that I should have
been warned how many times
I was ignorant to trust you.

Just like the sound of an a thousand
apples losing sight of their cores
during the autumn season,
I am watching the rest of what I knew
contribute to the process of elimination
when you persuaded everyone to believe
that I was as rotten as the apples
you find in inadequate grocery stores.

The difference is, I was never less than
a shimmer to those who were willing to
grasp onto the misconception that I was
more than a fragile human being that you
took the chances of sinking your teeth into.

It is now that I state that the ones like me
who are distinguished as delicious
and keen are the ones you should
think twice before considering that
I will be better tasteful if you intend bite me.

/ I have learned to bite back.

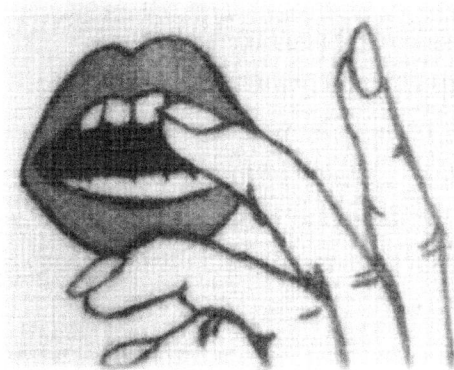

I remember one of the lovers I met
telling me that fate has a strange way
of letting us know the right timing.
For months leading into a year,
he would continuously stroll in and out of
my life like our friendship was a doorway to
a risk that if we went any further than
just enticing gazes listening
to each other's life stories -
It was like the closer we got, the more it felt
like two plugs being used in one single
socket; never having enough energy to store
for the both of us to actually keep working.

Or like those magnets you find in hardware
stores; you can attempt to try and force as
much pressure you want it to work but there
was never enough time in the world the
universe could have taken to
make us eventually attach to each other.
Simply because he was too infatuated with
the idea of fate and trying to fix what was
worth the many moments I spent
reminiscing us as more than just friends -

I was hardly able to feel the touch of his skin
and the way his body was almost like a
painting, keeping every single memory he
kept bottled inside of him
like each scar made to represent his story
but the one sliced across his face made me
attracted to him in a way where I became the
observer, spending months getting to know
him repeat all of his endless stories
he had spent his lifetime overcoming.

While keeping both ears open, I always had
to make sure to tape my eyes shut
because he would never hesitate to keep
reassuring me that we would always be
perfect for each other.
I had to force my eyelids from rolling back
into another unrealistic expectation doing
everything we said we could but in the end,
it was all the same old words.

So I smashed the windows and I broke the
handles on the back doors and I screamed at
the top of my lungs for letting the universe
keep cursing me forever letting me
get close to anybody anymore.

Somehow, I remain strong enough
to keep the world around me with a calm
state of mind yet also having the ability to
start hurricanes if you question my act
to think twice.

I believe now that I am capable of walking
through forest fires on my own.

I used to count every single bowling ball
even when I never knew how to get one
single strike when it came to successful
relationships, so I attempted to try and create
my own buildings and furnished towns with
my own toy blocks
and my collection of barbie dolls.

I used to write down letters to my future
husband as a little girl. I would draw stick
figures and accurately describe all the ways
I would be so eager to find the prince
charming in my fairytales.
I would come up with these unrealistic
stories and I would hide them in my secret
boxes placed in the corners of my
bookshelves and I would wish
on shooting stars the nights
I witnessed comets and constellations
that when I would find someone like you,
I would still think highly of our plotline
even after it was all over.

I guess you can say I have found the reason
as to why even in the most sanguine places
of my body there will still be a part of me
that always feels empty when the lovers they
chose as one-night stands or temporary
solutions became the partners they chose
to keep cherishing through every monthly
Instagram post –

I forgot to mention that I beg your pardon
but I am more than just a pretty face
for your amusement.
I am more than any flower
you happened to pick from a garden
I am more than competition, or even worse
I am more than just a second fucking option.

I am more than the tires on your vehicle
that takes you places you've
never even dreamed of,
I am more than a person who
gets to stand and watch you listen
I am more than entertainment or a song you
wrote about but never worth start recording.

I am more than just static on the radio,
I am more than just a single
text message every so often.
I am more than just a distant memory.
I am more than just the girl who fell in love
with the way you twitched in your sleep.
I am more than worthy enough to second
guess if I was ever in your dreams, so I hope
you started despising yourself when you
woke up for the fifth time
to get rid of the constant reminders that
I treated you *better* than anybody.

I am more than the shiver that breezes
through your windows, every endless and
sleepless night you kept praying you'll
forget about how ashamed you were to have
the ability to consider for any single second
that it was the right time to leave me.

I am more than the movies we watched
when you fell asleep on me,
I am more than the music you write,
I am more than the concrete you
continued to keep walking all over
because you kept telling yourself
it was okay to keep treating me
less than what I deserved.

I am more than the tears I shed questioning
if I was ever worthy of love,
I am more than the price of a ticket
not only to be placed on the back
but the front row of watching
each and every lover that I fought for
chase after those who did nothing to earn
any sort of type of chance
at a happily ever after.

I am still learning that maybe not everyone
I fall for deserves a place to call home.
In return, temporary moments are all
I get to keep when remembering why
the universe has made me cross paths
with so many different souls.

Perhaps I am not that girl
you meet next door,
I am the reflection of strength
that I had to fight for.
Which is why when I open mine,
my ears will pretend to listen to what you
have to say, but my heart is on mute
and when you begin to say the words you
wish to ask the girl who is too consumed in
her world of wanderlust located
in coffee shops and bookstores -
I will reply with the words
that I am the girl carving her own path
of self-love more than any god up above has
created for anyone else on this earth.
So I am warning you when you stumble
upon your path to find a brave soul like me,
I will say this -

I will be the thoughts that creep into the
cabinets of your head every morning you
awaken, you will have to remind yourself
in every possible way to keep them open
because I would rather be the girl you spoke
the truth to rather than dropping
grenades of guilt onto because I am not
designated to save you.
I am not the girl who will listen to your
repeated excuses when you start to presume
that I will always forgive you.
I am more than a person who deserves to be
trapped your thoughts so if you decide than I
am worth ungluing your lips shut -

I want you to tell me
I want you to show me
I want you to scream the words
when you're ready to fight for me
to step from this home I made out of my
own self-worth and prove to me the
presence of your soul is more
comforting than my own.

When you get the chance to trace your
fingertips over my delicate skin and
taste the words I leave on your lips -
the one and only thing I will ask of you
is to please

please

Never say the words

I love you.

Because I don't believe in them anymore.

/ What fate has taught me all these years

IV.

For the Saturating

139 | For Every Rose

But you see, there have been bad
things that stem from the good.
For the first time in a while,
I accepted that without being
frightened of the outcome.

I think that is the moment you realize
that you're going to be just fine.

All things make sense with reason;
It's okay not to be okay.
But we always forget that
It's okay *to be* okay as well.

We always lock the bad parts inside of our
heads, and when someone dares to question
it, we grasp onto the duct tape in fear they
will judge so we lock it in a storage room
only we are allowed to
make brief visits to but sometimes,
we end up trapping ourselves inside.
We are afraid that loving ourselves
despite what we have been
introduced to won't be the same –
perhaps it will be different
to watch the memories closest to us
begin to fade away when we allow
all the wrong paths to lead us to
the right destinations where we can
finally admit the words needed for our
lamentable souls -

I'm going to be alright.
I'm going to overcome this.
I'm going to be okay.
I need this.

/ Step One Of Recovery

I have come to establish with the ways
my feet have been scraping their paths
to get through too many filthy rock roads
as I persistently remind myself that
I deserve to keep paving through the
great number of splinters and blisters,
stepping in mud puddles and disastrous
cold weather that I will eventually
find something worthier than
what I have ever been given.

After a while, it seems my body
begins to feel just as jaded as the withered
leaves that find themselves too weak to stay
where they came from, so instead
they let the breeze take them

Sometimes, I like to compare myself not just
to the leaves that fall during the autumn
season, but I also consider myself some days
the trees that tend to let go of them as winter
returns -

Somedays I am the leaves that can still
make it with their ability to change colors.
Somedays I can appear that
bright and beautiful.
Somedays I allow the world to place me
where it faithfully wants me to.
But some days, I mostly end up feeling
as equally rigid and vacant as the wooden
trees who aimlessly stand and stare at the
world to show them that life is still meant
to be worth living when all it is somedays,
is you watching the world live without you.

/ Autumn has always been my favorite
season.

I am running out of time
reaching for every chipped piece of
these pinecones surrounding me

You see, I planted these trees around us
forbidding myself to do anything but grow
however, I failed to learn that maybe
that small ounce of reassurance
involving the idea of love
is just an endless journey to oneself,
maybe it's not about someone else.

These past few centuries it seems
to have left my bones - learning to love
again has developed into another false
diagnosis in these hospitals where I have to
force myself to keep trying to cure
my boredom within these puzzles
that never seem to fit anymore

So I twist and turn,
I break and I burn the memories
that get me to wondering which is stronger
hate over love or love over hate

Sometimes I think I do too much of both
perhaps I get an overload of one of the other
especially when it's all over
I am the world's biggest over exaggerator
of what I should keep together
in these empty chapters of stories
on these rotating bookshelves

As time continues on,
I find it increasingly difficult to fathom
the words framed in the corners of my brain
of all the letters I never sent
to those who I have spent
months mourning over seas
of possibilities that my curiosities
of them thinking about me
get the best of me.

This lake in front of me,
I grasp onto the dirt beneath me
and I adjust to the way
I am looking at it all differently

I am watching how the rain kisses
each lily pad delicately
I am watching at the tint of half of its body
transitions from smooth to gravitating

There are two types of lovers in this world
that I have come to swallow
down the fact I always perceived myself
as the stubborn one –

Playing games of scrabble,
shuffling over decks of cards
with the undeniable ability
to rid the moments
that mean the most

I told myself that I would *let go* of them
But it is until I step into a crowded room
the fluorescence of each light,
the scent of each perfume,
the taste of each careless being
that attempts to replace you -

I am nothing but selfish
because I have played one too many
games of battleship
since we left things unsaid.

I have learned to forgive,
but never forget the stories
I have yet to finish
so all I do, my friend
is glance periodically at these
blank pages as if they still mean
something when every introduction
begins with a different language
I no longer can interpret
why it all comes to an end

Therefore, I am the one girl
who rests in between every lover
in this world, desperately seeking slumber
in the gardens of these roses
changing from white to red
from red to black once summer has
faded to fall, and winter has made it
hard for me to make comfort
with awakening to the thought
of me with someone new

/ Pinecones

I remember the first time I fell in love.
I swear I could hear the forest singing
melodies of our wedding and how bright the
leaves glistened during daylight

It was easy to be in love with him.
But is love ever really meant to be easy to
begin with?

For it seemed I was always walking through
several paths where I left him behind only to
find myself on the repentant path of self-
destruction as the forest started to rain more
than it should have. I came across more than
a few snakes and sirens that caused me to
continuously look over my shoulder.
I could hear the crickets in the hours of
midnight, the wolves howling for their
partners and the animals that hid beneath the
tunnels

You screamed so loud that the trees began to
tremble, the branches began to deteriorate
from the forest fires you left when your
world began to turn into a natural disaster
You transformed the earth you knew into a
graveyard of long-lost lovers who made you
forget where you came from -
who pushed you this far to contemplate what
was worth staying alive for - those forest
fires you planted within your head
those thunderstorms that turned into
earthquakes that led you into multiple
different directions -

I remember the first time you felt cold
and your heart transitioned from red to blue,
your skin went from clear to bruised
and you started to make comfort with the
waves that crash among you -
Your fingers were starting to prune
your lips were turning purple
your eyes began to lose color
from the amount of times
you tried to breathe underwater

I remember how the ocean
felt like it listened to you
I remember how it had a way of soothing
your bones every thought, every path led to
the solution to keep staying where you made
comfort with never becoming warm again

But it's been almost two years and
you've managed to clear the waters
you've managed to dry your hair follicles
and dye it three different colors
You are stronger than
you ever have been
You are a goddess of love and compassion
You are the independent warrior you've
paved yourself through the trails of this
endless forest into a world of your own
self-appreciation and contentment.

You are you.
And that's all you can ever be.
You are more than extraordinary.
please believe me when I tell you
that no matter how tempting it can be,
Never lose faith in the pits of recovery.

/ *Stay Strong, beautiful.*

"Are you depressed?"

In hopes when I began to roll my eyes
towards the floorboards, they would
recognize how ignorant of a question that
was when precisely a week ago,
the lady dressed in black
ordered to keep track of every accident ever
made in our family's timeline
approached our front doorstep
and dared to spill the words out
like spoiled milk

Do me a favor and look up the definition.

Depression:
A mood disorder that causes a
persistent feeling of sadness
or loss of interest.
Often known in other words,
A mental illness.

I wanted to tell you that *I am getting better.*

By getting better, I mean I am still hanging
by the shoelaces dangling from the
streetlights during the midnight sky.
By getting better, I mean I am so numb to
the idea of embracing any type of emotion
as frozen as the icicles that hang from the
gutters behind the backdoors.
By getting better, I mean that I am still
endlessly suffering with the undeniable
desire to end what never was.

/ In other words (A Mental Illness.)

Maybe someday I will not remain as
the blank unwritten lines printed inside
every journal I have come to keep, perhaps
I would describe that as just how
growing up feels like -

Turning nineteen I would define as one of
my biggest accomplishments.
You see, nineteen was the year
I learned to finally be okay
with the weather changing sometimes.

I hope that you believe me when I say
that the only reason I refuse to stop racing
through deserted streets and flickering stop
lights, past the gardens of tulips, dandelions,
red roses and peaceful cemeteries is because
I am dangerously trying to neglect the girl
who attempted to plan her funeral over a
year ago.

Sometimes I look back onto old
photographs, ancient journal entries
and personal voice memos of myself
but little did I know that turning nineteen,
I allowed my own voice to become the
twisted turn of events where I started
relating with the way the seasons changed.

For instance, when I am sad,
I am the crickets during summer nights
I am the silence during long drives
However, when I am good -
I am equivalent to the bittersweet
refreshment of iced tea
or possibly the best scene played
at the end of your favorite movie.
When I am lovable,
I am the blanket you coat yourself
with during the winter
I am also the warmth of your delightful
 cup of hot cocoa
(with extra marshmallows)

In hopes you would understand that
I also have my days where I am not
readable.
I am not the iced tea on a hot sweaty day,
Most days, I am the fog after the rainstorms
Most days, I am not a cup half full instead -
I am the cup left half empty.

/ *Turning Nineteen*

Split branches
Fallen leaves
Different shades of green
I am leaving my trace
by stripping each rose petal
from its home

I am making my way
past the mud puddles,
the steep hills,
stepping from the bushes
tripping over logs -
keeping safe
from the weather

I venture this world I built
out of brick and stone
I taped the walls of this home
with words I had to reassure
the weather to stop becoming
a natural disaster

Sometimes when I speak to the earth
it talks back to me in
earthquakes and hurricanes
I tremble at its reaction of me
asking too much of it to
leave me alone without
causing another tornado

/ *When it gets too loud to handle*

I take these morning strolls
observing every cemetary of every
past lover and ask myself if it's possible
to mourn over your own tombstone

Little does anyone know that the soul
I did everything I could to write her off
each carved letter that sticks permanently
to represent she will always be there

Sometimes I recall standing in the rain
for far too long just to feel something more
than her call to save her

Sometimes I bury myself in other people's
graveyards because I prefer not to chase hers
anymore

To say the least, I am breathing
the most on the days I feel myself start to
hallucinate the moments I lose myself
in the beauty of the after life where
I am alive not just a ghost trying to
revive as the birds chirp
and the butterflies collide

I tell myself I am here for a reason

Pacing back and forth
shaking from head to toe,
the gardens I gather
with the intention of getting
to know the girl I ran from

I am kneeling down in front of her
every morning and every night
You shall find me rest a rose
beside her with a grain of salt
I coat in a circle

That's when I look up at the sky
when the moon is full, I don't
feel hollow at times because I
made it to the stars that shimmered
throughout the dark

/ *Overcoming*

IV. For The Awakened

Most days I am in my own head,
strolling through crowded towns,
capturing signs of every title,
every cafe and every piece of art I find

Once in a while, I stumble across
the idea of dating in this generation
is overrated with the romanticism
and unrealistic expectations.

As a writer,
I am capable of self-love,
but the idea of letting another person
peek through the hidden parts of my soul
I have yet to discover -
love is what I use to cherish
in the moments I share with lovers,
like empty coffee mugs,
crisped tongues each time
we allow ourselves to expect more

We're so accustomed to
the idea of someone staying
is rather too much to handle
because we're so used to taking care
of our own irreplaceable flaws

We don't expect others to accept them,
more than what we have grown to learn
But I am no longer scared, just rather
independently hesitant when it comes
to meeting someone different.

/ *Loving yourself first.*

"I love you,"
He claims, brushing his fingers against my
cheeks, staring me directly in both eyes
as if he expected me any sudden second to
cry

As if I was supposed to react differently
to the ways he could no longer filter himself
from replicating the same three words
overlapping until it vanished its own
visibility

I watched the clouds form around us
the cars and the outer world
kept moving forward except
he stood still frozen with the moon
that I captured still making itself permanent
next to the sun at twelve o'clock in the
afternoon

The fluorescence glistened
both shades of our eyes
I kept them locked on his, embracing myself
into igniting more than those words he kept
re-writing on blank pages to the chapters we
intended to read, disregarding my instincts
needlessly stripping themselves from head
to toe attempting to be vulnerable for him

For I should have seen it coming
when he scribbled out the characters,
sketching out the lovers he conjured
in his own lovesick delusions

I closed every book before you
could continue opening more

"You don't love me,"
I tossed the pages to the floor,
"You don't even know me,"
I scraped the match, inflaming
the crumpled papers into ashes

"How could you be so heartless?"
He fell down to his knees,
His hopeless expression questioning
every puzzle piece he kept scattered
to fit, like a key he kept buried to open
his heart too easily

Like it wasn't expected of me to
tell him the harsh reality

I observed the memories of us
he placed in his heart start to fall apart
I felt his skin start to singe at the flames
that traveled from the cement

His heartbeat raced a thousand miles
but his body could not find the energy to run
from the books he kept taped like
every girl he met had to play the right role

"I am not the girl you fell for."

I am the girl who narrates her own chapters,
I am the girl who snaps herself in and out of
her own delusions, administering myself
with the ability to enable every element
from air to earth
water to ice
energy to fire

I am the girl who gravitates through my own
directions with the journals I place in each
lesson kept stored in every coffin of my own
self kingdom –

I do not follow my heart or my head

I blink with both eyes
I walk with both feet
I cry until it's time to revive
my strength to say goodbye
to another lover who attempts
to rid me from my own sanity

/ *Walk Away*

There is a significant difference between
those infatuated with the curves of your
smile, the shape of your body,
and they will make an effort
to try and place their hands upon you,
and the next morning, it will all be over.
But it's the ones who make an attempt to get
to know your every detail of why you
admire those lyrics to that
favorite song of yours, or the reason why
you are so in love with being alone in your
own solitude of empty roads, passing cars
and never getting too close to the curbs
of every signal that
you don't deserve to feel this way forever.

*/ It's these ones you have to learn to stop
running faster from.*

People come and go like the sound of airplanes and helicopters you hear during the daylight. People come and go like the blurry outlines outside of train rides and gas stations. People come and go like the sound of static during the radio, and sometimes the song comes back on, but you missed the entire chorus because people come and go when they can't make a decision if you are important enough to permanently stay for. People are provisional it seems as you keep growing older so don't let yourself be fooled thinking you still miss them because deep down, it's just the mistake of wishing the memories you created could be re-made just because they tend to stick around longer than you wish.

/ *Learning to erase instead of replay*

The phrase *"everything is temporary"* was just as provoking as that one time the first time you went to therapy, and she gave you this cliché piece of advice to project yourself into this bubble so no one else can damage you with the demeaning insults that drove you here in the first place. You must have heard those three words countless times, it became tattooed in the fragments of your brain, yet you ferociously multiplied the times to look over it, because you payed more attention to keeping what was meant to be temporary, a permanent scar in your memories.

/ *Everything is temporary until you decide to let it go.*

Remember me
as the girl who taught herself to sing
who taught herself to tune every string
to the instruments that were too off key

Remember me
as the girl who learned to teach you
how to play with me

How to soak ourselves in the remedies
of our own sound of laughter,
thorough stories of the times
we needed an ear to listen to

Remember me as the girl
who held your hand,
the girl who could not keep herself
from dreaming of the day I'd find you

Remember me as your favorite scrapbook,
every candle and polaroid picture
I persuaded you to post as your wallpaper

Remember me as the girl
who spoke through the radio,
who cleared the roads
so you would not have to figure
out which was home

Remember me as the lighthouse
that peered in the center of the ocean
Remember me as the breeze
the echo of every sea shell

Remember me as the girl who fell
too deep for you
Remember me as the girl
who saved you from your own
hell you went back to

/ *When you chose someone new*

The first night in months
I managed to surface the fact
that I got to see you in my dreams again
I wouldn't call it a nightmare
but I didn't ask to be reminded of how
we left the arms of the clock tick tock

and *I know* that you're gone
I know it's been months
I know this room has been vacant
since we last spoke and
I know I've made it as far as
coming to terms that the moments
we spent are still stained in every
taste of the bitter sweetness
that steams from the coffee pot;

Like the faucet that drips on its own
when nobody is home and you're there
sitting on the kitchen counter wondering
if silence is supposed to bring peace,
why are my ears consistently ringing -

Sometimes I talk to myself
in different perspectives
whether it's the past,
Present or future tense

And if I could only go back
to the nights I was too unguarded to witness
that you had already moved on,
I would tell her to quit choking on her words
to tell you the unrequited truth

I would tell you that
it was not fair to tell me
to close the door
to shut the curtains
and change the channels

I would tell myself to stop
overlooking all the ways it revealed
red flags and obligated mixed signals

I would beg her to take note
on every light bulb that blew out
at the uncalled-for conversations
at 2 am when she flooded the floors
with questions why you never would
stay for much longer

I would tell her to start fighting for herself

I don't deserve you
I don't deserve you
I don't deserve you

You don't deserve me
for sacrificing months to an eternity
longing to swallow down this untainted
coffee that you are doing better off
without me

I take note to wait for the mornings
I awaken to let the caffeine cool down
before it leaves my taste buds crisped
and my hands too weak to hold
the appetite of you to become savoring

I keep reassuring myself that it was not my
fault for how many times it took to convince
my heart that I can taste other flavors
sometimes
I can track the scent of the same words you
said and pretend that maybe they mean
something

As long as they are forbidden
to be stated in the past tense

/ The selfish act

I am gazing at him
from across my seat
I am playing the piano
with each finger tip
as if the world has eased
itself at our windshield

I am blinded by the light
I am squinting too much
to realize that he is passing
every red light and every stop sign

I tell him I should drive
He smirks a gentle smile
as if he could be any less concerned

I am observing his lips curve
vocalizing that I am his favorite girl

Except the more I hear him,
the glass around us begins to shatter

I attempt to renunciate the words
that used to come out like the sound
of a thousand hummingbirds
when the sky was clearer

I tell him that we should remember
the road we came from -
we should remember to be safer

He fails to care about every flat tire
that catches the potholes,
He forgets to pull over at the sirens
chasing behind us

I demand him to stop the car
He takes another exit off the road
as we land somewhere far in the woods
abandoned in the middle of a thunderstorm

I reach for the handles, I let out my hand
I manage to step into quicksand
when he no longer pays attention
to the fact that I am sinking

And he does not seem to catch me

Instead he just faces me,
and I am left wondering why
I couldn't tell he was the one
manipulating every element of the earth
in the first place

/ *Natural disasters*

185 | For Every Rose

Darkened branches reaching
from every tree that stands around me
Every fallen leaf covering the shades
of each flower that made its way to radiate
positivity yet I am unconsciously stepping
over each petal across the wet patches of
grass

Somehow, I recognize the reflection
of the spirit I buried beneath
staring despondently back at me

Mud puddles and steep hills -
I occur in different aspects of this world
where I do my best to avoid every
signal of her to entangle me into her
footsteps

I venture this universe I assembled
to recover from each wound
I constructed it to survive through
the spontaneous weather and temperatures
unlike her - who was too weak to lift a
finger

She thrived on grief and emotional turmoil
and I made certain I twisted my mindset to
a different outlook of talking back to the
world in earthquakes and hurricanes –
I wished to see the beauty
and ignite every beautiful fragment of it

Would you believe me if I told you
that I am made more of pale skin,
amber eyes and chestnut brown hair?

Would you believe me if I died it red
to rid the afterlife of the girl who let herself
drown in others opinions and criticism?

Would you agree with me that sometimes
home is not the most comforting
to seclude to?

Would you call me crazy if I admitted that
I would rather remain a mystery to those
who perceive me as the girl who smiles too
often, laughs at everything

Would you call yourself a stranger
in your own body?

Would you want to stay for the ending
if you knew all I have endured are
beginnings?

Would you be convinced that I am most
likely abusing these words you speak to
formulate my own hand-written letter I
eventually seem to make
the day you decide to escape?

I take these morning strolls
calculating every cemetery I stumble across
I count the tombstones of every lost lover
I stored in every coffin to mourn from
but little was I aware of my own
I cannot seem to visit too often

I am not afraid to be left anymore
But I am deadly frightful of that one
specific graveyard of the girl I used to know
the girl who put up with every past lover

I had to bury them
I tell myself the days I recall
standing face to face in the rain
for too long just to feel more
than the chill of her touch

I had to bury you
I assure her it was not my fault
until I begin to pace back and forth
anxiously shaking from head to toe

The soul I absorbed prior
has made itself at home
inside the holes I feel pouring
themselves out the days I
let her in somehow

Every morning and every night
you shall find me placing every rose petal
I keep with a grain of salt circulating
each coffin I dug deep enough
to prevent from re-opening

That's when I glance up at the sky most
nights and the moon is full, not as hollow for
once in my life because I made it to the stars
that shimmer this time when I ask of them if
I will feel better

I talk to the clouds that confine every
released emotion every wander less
thought and lonely feeling
I transition into different shapes sometimes
depending on the way you decide to
distinguish me

As a fair warning,
when you find me in the spring
I will not shower over your land
I may just spread more of myself over
each garden to leave you a trace
of the star that defined her own

/ *Past lives*

191 | For Every Rose

Faded letters
like a stone carved into bark
of the tree that makes you
who you are -

Please never be repentant
of the roots that were born to grow

You are more powerful
than you know

You are a warrior
build out of bricks
and tenderhearted petals
that broke from their stems

You are still beautiful
inside and out

You are wonderfully made
in every landscape of art
that you trap yourself
inside every coffee shop
museums and art shows

You are your own self desolation
formed out of aesthetic paint brushes,
too many scribbled sketches
of multiple attempts to trace yourself
into perfection

You are nothing but articulate to those
who refuse to recognize
the themes worth reading
the stories you keep concealing
But it does not matter
because those who cannot decipher
every flaw, every mark
every portrait or unrestrained thought

They do not deserve
a second of your attention
if they dare to say anything less
of how incredibly elegant you are

/ *Despite every scar*

It may seem like the world is against you,
Like your bedroom walls are closing in on
you.

It seems your own place you turn to
when it doesn't reply with an answer to all
your issues, and maybe that's why you talk
to it so much.
Because you are too disguised by your own
lies that you are too terrified to tell anyone
how bad it really intensifies when you are
too consumed in every horrid flashback, so
you attempt to write them out.
Even when you're alone in your own world
crashing down over your shoulders,
Even when struggling to make it through the
suffocation of your own intoxication of
panic attacks and mental breakdowns,
let it happen.

Let the waves crash against your skin,
But don't make comfort with it.

/ Letting It In

You cannot escape the past.
You cannot escape the nostalgia
disguised in late night car rides
when that one specific song plays
and brings you back to that one time
of when things were better with them.
You cannot escape the missing
of wish they were still there.
You can only hope that life
worked its way out for a reason.
And that one is obvious enough,
You just have to face it.
You have to keep going on without them.

/ Letting It Go

There are segments of my body
some more substantial than the rest
He asked me why did I give him a taste
if I never planned on giving him
the entire map to coordinate the paths
it would take past the front porch step

I told him once you dig yourself in
there is no going back
These sections of my soul
I earned with my own tainted brush

I do not allow them
to be cherished by anyone else

As he tilted his head in concern,
I placed my lips onto his
planting visions of ghost towns
countless gardens
that are replenished by
the waterfalls I created
inspired through my wars
against myself

I told him I found hope in the rivers
I told him I made it to the surface
After years of debating whether
I should sink or swim

And I do not wish
anyone to unravel
these places I stepped foot in
on bare feet just to breathe again

He takes my hands
and he pulls me into his chest

I can hear his heart beating
I can feel the both of us
start to sink like quick sand
I find myself losing
control of my well being
my fingers pruning,
my lips chapping,
my makeup smearing

I tell him I can handle myself
that I do not wish anyone to
take care of my over dwelling thoughts
and contemplations if you will
last longer than the rest

I tell him thank you for the
moments we spent
I tell him I do not need them
to feel less vacant in the parts
of my heart I've kept shut

He thinks he is worthy of
untying every pattern
every rope I strapped
forbidding anyone to unfasten

I chuckle gripping onto the hands that bind
He no longer manages to dig deeper
when he loses sensation in his fingers

/ *Protecting myself*

There are sections of life that
will break you down.
They will sink their teeth into
the pores of your skin
and they will constantly remind you why it's
so hard to forget of everything that can go
wrong from then on -
but you have to embrace the little things
that make life a little bit more interesting.

Remember the lady who smiled at you
in the grocery store.
Make a little reminder in your notes
to stay strong.
Compliment the color of someone's
favorite eyeliner.
You can still find the light of what life fails
to give you sometimes.

/ *The Little Things*

Everyone at a young age likes to believe
they are certain that we all have an accurate
goal of where we see ourselves
in ten years, or at least how we're going to
get there. We all have this pressure before
graduation high school what our parents, our
aunts and uncles, or even distant cousins
will perceive us if we want to say
"I don't know yet,"
to their questions of what we're passionate
about at family reunions.

It's okay to take time to figure yourself out.
It's more than logical enough to be placed
on a map life has made unclear to you, but
don't stay in one spot for too long because
you are afraid of the unknown.

Take risks. Cross paths.
Experience opportunities,
learn which one you're
most influenced from.
Then go from there.

/ Being patient with yourself

You are more than entitled to give yourself
credit for putting up with all the bullshit.
You are more than enabled to give yourself
the rest you rid the nights they left you for
somebody else.
You are more than allowed to fall in love
with every flaw they never could.
You are more than qualified to be given the
Opportunity to find happiness even when it
feels like they never let go of the purpose
but made the marks to prevent you from
moving on.

You are still a human being without them.
You are still beautiful, you are still worthy,
You are still enough for yourself.

Please, believe this even when
they have left you again.

Please love yourself to the point where it is
believable that you no longer needed them
to begin with.

/ Reassurance

Everyone has this misconception of
recovery,
claiming that the beginning of changing
one's ability to loving themselves is an
overnight transition,
but let me tell you something, my friend -
Recovery is a constant change of mindset.
Recovery is something you cannot take
back.
Recovery is just as unfortunate as the
multiple fixations a vehicle gets hit with no
matter how much fortune you recently spent
on it.
My father as a child, even my mother would
always ask me if I was alright or if I was
better. Truth be told, I was never close to
the lies I spoken from my mouth.

Recovery is reassurance from yourself -
whispering to the parts of your soul
that you were too frightened to confront.
Recovery is you telling yourself
you can get through it.
Recovery is taping those
journal pages back together
because you were too outraged
to even write them out
so you tore them apart to
help you feel better.
Recovery is soaking that towel on the floor
of maybe those one, or two,
or hundreds of cups of tea
you knocked over the nights it got too hard,
but instead of letting it stain the floorboards,
You chose to clean it up
with that paper towel.
because at least you're
doing something
to make it better.

If there is one thing in this life I could
spread across the skies,
If there is one thing I could paint on
everyone's front door
and help them realize that there are so many
problems that are going in this world, yet no
one willing to listen to them,
I would scorch the words into their heads
that everyone is human.
We all have our ways of coping with the
anxiety on a day to day basis.
We shall not judge each other for our
mistakes,
We should never allow our ways we used to
rid our sadness
to cloud the more alternative coping
mechanisms that we can still recover.
We can still be better than
what we settle for.
Please believe that mental illness is
something we cannot change,
It is something we cannot differentiate,
but it is something we can adjust to living
around to where it is nothing
but a distant echo in the background.

You have to keep fighting.

You have to believe you are worth recovery.
I am begging you to trust the strength you
were given to endure
the grief, you can allow yourself to fight for
the release of
all the pain you let yourself become
accustomed to.
Please, fight for recovery even when it
seems to fail you.
Because recovery is not the failure, it is you
that needs to face
what is realistic, and that is not letting
yourself be destroyed forever.
You can overcome this, and you will
survive.

Recovery is never chosen, because recovery
is never given enough credit that it is the
solution to escaping the forests and the
mental institutions –

Recovery is never a failure to you.

Recovery is what makes you into the
garden that grows outside during the 365
days of a year.
It is the garden that keeps sprouting
throughout the seasons, but you don't even
know that even when you feel like you're
not even living, you're just existing,
take note of the fact that
even when you feel like you are still
suffering - you are still those dandelions
outside your front porch still having the
energy to become elegantly relevant
when the summer comes, even during
downpours –

You are still in charge of your own kingdom
of lovely flowers and shades of the weather
and how much you can endure.

Recovery is a constant adjustment to keep
growing up until before you know it,
You are the goddess of freedom
and you made it past the lessons,
and the mood swings of the weather.

You are still here. And you are still lovely.

Keep breathing.
Keep changing.
Keep fighting.
Keep choosing
to keep
recovering.
Because it is so
worth it,
just as much as
you are too.

About The Author

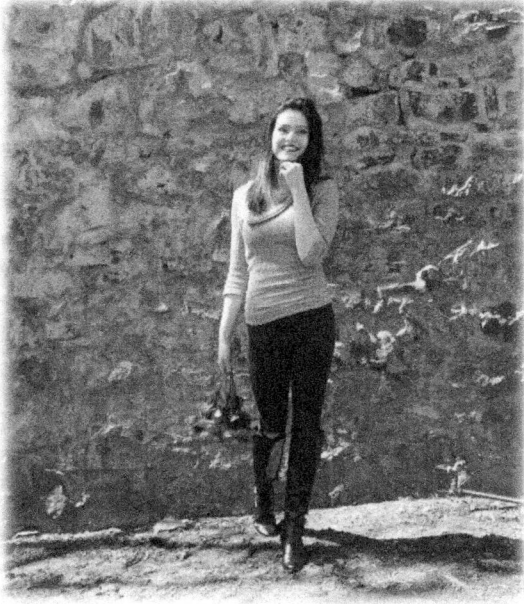

20-year-old Isabelle Sousa was born
back in September of 1998.
She lives in Connecticut with her family.
She majors in psychology and creative
writing, in addition to being inspired
to put this entire book of her personal pieces
of writing altogether.

Since the second grade,
she had found her interest in writing,
keeping journals since age fourteen,
and writing poetry since she was sixteen.

She is now dedicated to publishing one of
her passions, in hopes her words may reach
out, relate, and inspire those
who have been through the same
experiences.
These are the many pieces she decided to
share about through the dreadful heartaches,
lessons learned, letters to past lovers
and her messages about mental illness,
staying strong,
and fighting to always better yourself.
This is her at her most vulnerable, pure and
raw form, sharing her deepest buried
thoughts, past self-inflicted battles
that it took these past two years in recovery
to overcome in which she's never revealed
to anyone up until now

I want to take the time to thank everyone who supported me into getting this out there.

My best friends since high school. My parents. My family. Even the strangers or closest co-workers who I get to listen to every morning at my job who give me a reason to smile every day. I want to thank my lovely photographer Katerina, (Drake Photography) who helped capture every photo attached inside.

But most importantly, I want to thank you for taking the time to read my story. I only hope you can take mine as an inspiration to keep writing yours. Keep inspiring yourself through something you're passionate about.

I hope you all find yourself someday if you haven't already yet.
If you are on your way, keep heading towards it.
If there's anything I wish any one of you to grasp from this book is to keep cherishing life even if you don't have the strength sometimes.

You deserve to find happiness within yourself. Keep embracing every flaw. Keep loving yourself first no matter what.

I remember the nights I never thought
facing myself in the mirror
wouldn't be a struggle.
I remember the nights
I wanted it all to be over.
I remember the pain. I remember the hurt.
I remember the girl I was before.

If I am most thankful for anything
at all in this world,
I am thankful for her
Because without her,
I would never have the ability
to overcome every feeling
that inspired me to turn
my story into something empowering.

Without her,
I would never be as
pure, raw, and capable
of cherishing myself in every possible way
I spent my entire life reaching.

You can get there, love.
I promise you.

Isabelle Marie

Thank you for taking the time to read my story that I turned into an art after years of writing. I only hope you ~~house~~ cherish what you love the most as well. We all have our stories so be proud of yours. Stay positive and keep staying bright as the person you are.

thank you

28211038R00117

Made in the USA
Columbia, SC
09 October 2018